The Colored Girl Beautiful

The Colored Girl Beautiful

Emma Azalia Hackley

MINT EDITIONS

The Colored Girl Beautiful was first published in 1916.

This edition published by Mint Editions 2021.

ISBN 9781513223025 | E-ISBN 9781513221526

Published by Mint Editions®

MINT
EDITIONS

minteditionbooks.com

Publishing Director: Jennifer Newens
Design & Production: Rachel Lopez Metzger
Project Manager: Micaela Clark
Typesetting: Westchester Publishing Services

Contents

Foreword

This volume has been compiled from talks given to girls in colored boarding schools. The first talk was given at the Tuskegee Institute at the request of the Dean of the Girls' Department.

It was an impromptu talk after an hour's notice. Just before the Dean closed the door to leave me alone with the girls, I repeated my question, "What shall I talk about?" The reply was, "Tell them anything you think they should know. They will believe an experienced woman like you who travels and knows the world and life."

As I looked at the sea of faces, "wanting to know," and as I thought of all they had to learn, the vastness of all of it almost overpowered me. "May I sit down, girls? Now, what shall we talk about that is interesting to everyone of you?"

"Would you like to talk about Love—real Love?" "Yes, yes," came the answer. "Would you like to talk about Beauty—real Beauty?" "Yes! Yes!" they answered and the chairs were pulled forward. For forty minutes we had a heart to heart talk. The dean and teachers had perhaps told the girls the same words, but the message seemed to come more directly to them from one who had daily contact with the great, busy world.

The talks were very informal and personal and as the girls asked questions the thought came to me to jot down the points, that similar talks might be given to the girls in other schools. Then came the request, "You come so seldom, can you print the talks?" Much of the talks could not be printed because many of the questions and answers were personal.

If I had a daughter I would desire that she should know these things and more, that she might be a beacon light to her home and to the race. As I have not been blessed with a daughter, I send these thoughts to the daughters of other colored women, hoping that among them there is some new thought worthy of a racial "Amen."

E. Azalia Hackley
Chicago, Ill., August, 1916

The Future

The beautiful part about the colored race in America, is the future. As a mixed race we are undeveloped. We may become whatever we WILL to become.

This race is a growing people. The future is veiled but it may reveal some strange things to the world. What opportunities there are for leadership! If there were only some ways to "squelch" the fakers and arouse the dreamers!

If each would only think out a different plan for race advancement, there would always be followers. Some would be attracted in one way and others reached in another way, and so carry lines of thought.

The gardener is aiming towards better vegetation. Scrubs and dwarfs are sacrificed totally to produce a more perfect plant.

The horse breeder, any animal breeder, the bird fancier, all aim to get a better breed of stock in each generation.

The cry of the hour is "A better breed of babies." As it takes several generations to breed a prize winner, it is time for the colored race to look into these things and prepare for the future colored child, handicapped as it will be. Nature needs assistance in this.

Attractiveness in appearance is a strong factor in success. A pleasing, even, charming personal appearance may be cultivated.

The mind—the gray matter—either fills the body with life or beauty, or it destroys life and beauty, according to the concentration of thought, and resulting habits.

If one were to ask, "Can a leopard change its spots," the reply must always be, "No." But if one were to ask if the Negro could change his appearance, through himself, his own will power, the answer would be, "Yes," because the Negro has a thinking brain. He may become as attractive as he wills to become.

As his taste and ideas of beauty conform to the accepted, so will he grow like these ideals and standards.

The Colored Child Beautiful

Every baby is beautiful to its mother. Every colored baby is generally, only cunning or cute to many of the white race who have their own ideal of baby beauty, which depends mainly upon a white skin.

Beauty is a matter of personal opinion. To a savage African, a baby with a black skin and flat nose is the ideal.

To a Chinese, a plump, yellow, slant eyed baby satisfies.

To the Esquimaux, the round faced, small eyed, black haired little one is the admired type.

A child should be taught to love and be proud of its race and to know the good points of the race.

Colored babies are born with rare physical gifts. First: They are born with the most beautiful eyes in the world. Unlike foreign children who come to this country, they seldom have sore eyes. I have visited about six hundred colored schools and have yet to see a sore eyed colored child.

The obligation of a gift is the preservation and cultivation of this gift. Little colored children should be taught to keep their eyes open and bright with intelligence and clear with good health, because the eyes are the windows of the soul. Their eyes should look straight into the eyes of others with their souls shining through. Their eyes must be kind eyes, listening eyes, observant eyes, thoughtful eyes, and remembering eyes.

Second: Colored people are credited with having the finest teeth in the world. The obligation of this gift is cleanliness and preservation of this attractive gift. A colored child should be taught to deny herself to pay a dentist's bill.

Third: Colored people have the finest voices in the world. The obligation of this gift is its cultivation, proper care and control of the voice, and to speak in good English.

There are other natural gifts but of them—later on. The greatest gift to the Negro is himself. So much in him is hidden, spiritually, intellectually, psychically and physically, that he is a vast unexplored mine.

All colored babies like all little white babies, excepting in the shades of color, are born about alike, with round or long heads, all with the same soft spot on the crown, and like white babies, are mostly all mouth because they are hungry little animals and use their mouths often.

As the child observes, thinks, and "wills," the bumps and hollows appear, the features develop and lines grow. Any ugly little baby may develop into a beautiful child. Any beautiful child may grow ugly and coarse.

If babies were born with developed features they would be monstrosities.

"Within each of them is an inward sculptor, Thought, who is a rapid, true workman."

Colored children should be taught that Thought will improve their good points and will eradicate any objectionable points. They should be taught their good points and their bad points, and should be encouraged to improve their personal appearance, as far as objectionable racial characteristics are concerned.

As the girl grows she should be taught the value of personal appearance as a factor in her life problem and ultimate success.

A little colored girl who wants to be pretty should be taught what "pretty" really is. The old proverb says, "Pretty is as pretty does," thus recognizing the power of the inward Sculptor Thought, and its controlling and cultivating forces.

At an early age the child should be given subjects to think about. She should be taught to see the beautiful in Nature and Art that the reflection may be seen in her face and in her actions. Ask her if she saw the sun rise this morning or the sun set last night, or if she noticed the moon light, or the grandeur of the low black clouds, or the fleeciness of the soft white clouds; tell her to listen to the language of the birds and insects, and the sighing of the winds through the trees. Tell her to listen to the teeming of the earth and ask where and when the earth smells the sweetest. Teach her to walk and talk with Mother Nature and to recognize her voice in everything, until Nature will appear more, mean more, and teach more. Companionship with flowers and the cultivation of plants is to be recommended, even in the most congested flat life.

The colored child should be taught Negro History that she may be proud of her dark skin. It is a long interesting story way back to the days of Ethiopian glory, for the Negro is the sub-strata of that race. Tell the child how fair races from the North invaded Africa, and until today the present colored race can trace its black blood back to African kings and queens, and its white blood to the kings and queens of the Old World.[1]

---

1. The Bible and other books tell us that the Ethiopians were a prominent people before the time of Christ.

Recently in excavations pictures of Egyptian princes reigning 2900–2750 B. C. prove from their hair that they had Negro blood. America will have these proofs in the Boston Museum of Fine Arts.

Let her know that the black man was the author of much of the world's history, and that Moro, the capital of Ethiopia, was at one time the great seat of learning. She should be taught early in life to read Ancient History, that she may see what the black man has done for the world, that she may have pride in her black blood as well as in her white blood. Tell her the record of the Negro as a soldier, statesman, and explorer. Read to her about the brave part that he played in the war of 1812 and subsequent wars, even in the recent terrible war, he was among the bravest. Help her to make a scrap book that she may pass her knowledge on to others. While authorities in history say that a race once great, can never attain greatness again, as truly as the pendulum swings this mixed race will surely come into its own. The colored race comes from several lines of white ancestry, and as fruit is grafted to a finer degree of species, so the colored race will some day show its latent powers. The child of today is to be the mother of the great child that is to be, and each one must do her part to help prepare for the future great colored child.

Teach the colored girl about prejudice. Parents should read up the World's history of persecution and note the accounts of race and religious persecution in England, France, Germany, Russia, Turkey and Spain. Even today there is English hatred of the East Indian, Russian persecution of the Jew, and Turkish persecution of the Armenians. Then, too, Europeans are only just beginning to regard the Oriental nations as human beings. Prejudice is hard to explain and hard to conquer. It has taken generations in other instances and the world has always kicked the under dog. Tell the colored child how these other persecuted nations are conquering prejudice; tell her that each colored child must be a race missionary and prove her worth and powers, thus winning friends for the race.

She must be taught the application of the story of Esther to her race. Tell her that each colored girl may be an Esther, especially in all matters of cleanliness, manners, and self sacrifice, to advance and change the prevalent opinion of the Negro. Each colored woman, not only bears her own burden, but she bears the burden of posterity and the burden of the race. Each one must fit herself for the triple burden. Not even a talent should be used wholly for personal gain nor solely for present uses. Her education must be a process of development of powers not only to fit her for citizenship and life, but it must fit her for her race's burdens.

EMMA AZALIA HACKLEY

Someone has said:

"To educate a boy is but the education of an individual—but when one educates a girl, the education of a family results."

Every little colored girl, like every little white girl, wants to be beautiful. What is beauty? Beauty is a combination of personal appearance and charm, and it can not be purchased.

Each year the merchant takes stock and separates all the best articles, the medium articles, and the poor articles.

And so when one determines upon self improvement, she should take stock. She sums up her good points and her bad points. The good points she will accentuate and the bad points she will eradicate, unless Thought, the inward Sculptor has been at work too long. It is for this reason that little colored children should be taught early in life to think rightly.

"As the sprig is bent, so will the tree be."

Every thought, every emotion has an outward manifestation. Because people think, feel, and act, they leave marks of these in bodily lines and habits. Not only is the face a bulletin board, but as Schopenhauer says, "One's life may be his autobiography." One's life may even be read from his skeleton.

Sometimes certain thoughts and habits repeated and repeated leave spots. Spots always depreciate whether on wool, meat, wood, animals or people. Has the Negro any "Spots"? Other people think so. If these so-called "spots" will interfere with his future success in life then let him eradicate them with the inward Sculptor—Thought.

Is the dark skin a spot? Oh no, it is his history, his strength, as was Samson's hair. Because of his color he has powers and forces which could get him anything he desires in life if he would only begin while a child, to learn restraint, how to govern and control himself until he could accumulate sufficient will power to direct these forces for his own advancement.

Because of his color he has rare psychic powers which are not yet understood by himself or by the world.

What is the largest Spot? If one wishes to get a true estimate of himself he finds out what others ridicule concerning him.

What feature about the Negro is ridiculed the most? Why, the mouth. What is the matter with it? A large mouth is supposed to be the sign of generosity. No, but if it has thick lips and is a leaking mouth? If it hangs open too much? Only two classes of persons are excused from having open mouths, and these are children with adenoids and imbeciles. Everyone else is supposed to keep his mouth shut most of the time.

The leaking mouth with the hanging under jaw causes a tendency to "leak" along other lines. One's business and personal affairs "leak" in street cars, public places, and on the streets to the detriment of the race.

Permitting the lips to hang, thickens them. They grow too heavy to hold up. Too much grinning and loud laughter will widen the mouth and loosen it. We do not desire small mouths, but we do not look attractive with "leaking mouths." Our mouths are improving. In the schools and college pictures we find unmistakable evidence that Thought is working wonders with the Negro mouth.

What is the next most ridiculed "Spot"? The nose. What is the matter with the noses? Large noses are said to be an indication of character and ability. Napoleon always selected the generals with large noses because he believed them to be more efficient. Oh, but the noses are often flat and have no hump.

Look at the hump of the Roman nose which indicates "fight." Look at the hump of the Indian nose which also indicates warlike tendencies. Take the Jewish nose. The hump means fight—a continual warfare for gold.

But the Negro has been a peaceful person, consequently he developed no nose hump. It is time that he developed a hump—a Negroid hump. He must pinch up, think up, will up, a hump. The time has come to fight, not only for rights, but for looks as well. He must build up a nose with more character, which can not be ridiculed. Grinning widens the nose and prevents its upward building, so grinning must cease.

In examining the pictures of graduates from the different schools, we find that Thought is changing the noses as well as the mouths. As the mouth and nose are changed, so will the whole expression of the face be changed.

The Negro's hair may be considered a "Spot" by some, but care and cultivation are changing this so-called "Spot" and more care and attention will work more wonderful results.[2]

---

2. "Kinky hair is neither a disgraceful nor a shameful heredity. It is an honorable legacy from Africa. A kind Mother Nature protected her children from the torrid sun which kept the oils and waxes in a fluid state or else the hair would have dried up. The chemical action of the atmosphere caused a shrinking into spirals which further protected the uncovered heads from scorching."

Constant care of the hair will cause an improved condition of the texture which will in time be inherited.

EMMA AZALIA HACKLEY

His eyes and his teeth are good points and he has been given a magnificent backbone as well as a beautiful voice, although he often permits these gifts to degenerate.

Because God has given each colored girl a beautiful voice, she should be taught to speak in a soft mellow tone. She should speak eloquently and elegantly. If she screeches or yells and abuses her vocal cords, she will not only disgust people but she will lose her voice and have no beauty of tone to bequeath.

As the colored child has been made in the image of God, her poise should be erect and fearless. Nature bestowed the gift of a straight backbone.

The native African has always been straight like the pine sapling. In civilization his descendant permits his back to bend. The chest caves in, squeezing the heart, lungs and liver. One is more liable to pneumonia and tuberculosis, and can not fight them successfully as these organs have lost much of their vital force because of their cramped conditions.

Power is expressed in the way one carries her shoulders, and vitality is measured by breathing capacity.

One may sin against God and be forgiven, but Mother Nature never forgives the sin against her. Unto the third and fourth generation the punishment goes on for the abuse of the temple of the Soul.

E very colored girl would like to be beautiful. The so-called beauty is but skin deep. A burn, a scar, a disease, and beauty is fled, although contour and other evidences might remain.

One can not remove bad looks with soap and water. Youth should be and is always attractive. It is after twenty-five that one begins to wish that she had been more careful in her youth, that she had controlled her powers, and that she had cultivated her good points and removed her "Spots."

A girl should study herself, learn her powers, and she will get the real beauty if she will deliberately and persistently train for it.

We look at the photos of beautiful, smiling, round-faced children and then at the tired, many-lined unhappy faces into which they have changed. Women delight in showing us photos to prove how beautiful they were when they were sweet sixteen. As we look, it is hard to believe. However, the camera, they say, always tells the truth, and we have later evidence before us.

The inward tools, Thoughts, have carved the ugly pictures on faces. Ignorance is a terrible curse along all lines. Many have not learned the secret of preserving their bodies, along with other studies, yet the savage nations care for their bodies.

Girls abuse their bodies; they eat too much or else the wrong kind of food, causing indigestion or other stomach and liver troubles. There is no room for the distended digestive organs and gorged stomachs and if these walls are stretched too often they lose their elasticity and the digestive juices go on a strike, causing eruptions on the face and a bad complexion, besides other complications which destroy beauty. Then, too, coarse or highly seasoned foods arouse other appetites through the law of sympathy.

Girls do not heed the signs of colds and complications peculiar to women. Operations are often necessary because of exposure and neglect of colds. The clothing is often too tight and pressure causes malignant growth and great suffering in after years.

A girl should keep her face as clean as a man's face after shaving, and her body should be correspondingly clean, that the gases and odors may escape, lest they take revenge upon her face. A girl should no more offer a foul odor of body or mouth or nose, than she would offer poison.

A girl must study her body and preserve it by attending to colds and diseases in time.

One who desires beauty should fight against a desire for intoxicants. There is nothing that coarsens the skin of some women so quickly as the habit of drinking beer. Chewing gum coarsens the muscles of the jaw and gives a downward trend that few faces can afford to wear.

The real beauty is carved from within and the inward Sculptor is always at work. One may buy artificial teeth, hair and limbs, but no cosmetics or massage will cover up the ravages of Thought. Every thought leaves its imprint and every emotion leaves its manifestation.

Beauty is not always a tangible something. Many people are called beautiful when they do not even own attractive features. Charm and personality throw a special light over the features, thus transforming them. Anyone may cultivate charm and personality if she has not been born with them.

To be beautiful, one must fill her mind with beautiful thoughts. Impure thoughts, angry thoughts, unhappy thoughts, jealous thoughts, and cowardly thoughts will arise, but they must be driven away. Health suffers from these thoughts because they affect sleep and appetite. Lines appear upon the face as an index of interior troubles.

One must not only be careful of thinking detrimental things, but she must be careful of what she says to others, and of what she writes in letters, for writing a thought intensifies its influence.

Impure novels often lead girls astray or give them impure thoughts which are printed or published in their faces.

A girl should not affect boldness. It "sets" the muscles in the face and neck. One should affect modesty and purity even if one does not feel them, that they may enhance her looks.

Rough uncouth actions and gestures cause ugly lines in the face.

Not only is the face the bulletin board of habitual thought, but the body reflects thought through gestures and other movements.

Repose of manner and a soft voice are two of the greatest charms that a woman may possess. Restlessness is not only a sign of lost control, it gives a false idea to passers-by. Quietude gives a sense of power. Control is culture, and culture is a beauty point.

Someone has said that in the matter of first impression, "appearance is half and the voice is the other half." "Later you will be able to make one forget an unattractive appearance, but we never grow accustomed to a rasping voice." "Nothing in the world is so humiliating as to be a graceful and beautiful woman with a bad voice."

Talkativeness is another "Spot," and a sign of lost control. In public places, especially, it is a sign of ill breeding and bad taste. Good breeding should always keep a woman from loud talk. We must remove the stigma of loudness and coarseness that now rests upon the race. The less a person knows, the bigger noise she generally makes. The big touring car never makes the noise that a motor cycle does, nor does a great steamer make the fuss that a tug boat does. The deep stream is silent while the little brook babbles.

It is exceedingly vulgar to air one's opinions in street cars, railroad cars, or in any public place. A person who really knows anything does not parade his knowledge or his opinions.

While emotional people are generally attractive, yet the habit of the expression of the emotions could be turned to better account.

Lost Motion and Lost Emotion are the two great "wastes" of the race.

One not only enhances her beauty but one is really a Somebody or a Nobody according to the control she has over her mind and body. She must control her emotions as she does her appetite. Excessive emotion debilitates the system. Anger is poison to a woman's system. It causes a chemical action which upsets the stomach. The bite of an angry person is sometimes poisonous, because of this chemical change. A fit of anger may upset the whole digestive system, and may even cause death because blood is taken from the digestive system and many bodily functions cease. Any emotion causes the heart to beat faster.

There is health as well as beauty in self control. Culture is self control. The Colored Girl Beautiful should cultivate reposefulness. A display of emotion or restlessness indicates lost control.

There are only two classes of people who are excusable for disturbing large quantities of air in their movements. These are babies and lunatics, because neither have brain development nor mental control.

The colored girl beautiful must learn to sit still. She must learn to be methodical in order to have resting periods. She needs a few minutes each day for relaxation and repose. If she has not learned to relax, she should change her occupation at different periods of the day. She must train herself not to get excited. She must not quarrel or argue. She must train herself to be temper-immune, and not to permit others to upset her equilibrium.

A real lady never gets visibly angry. Anger drives away friends who really help to make us beautiful by giving us pleasant sensations.

One should be eternally feminine. One should not attempt athletics unless she is sure that her physique will endure this. A strain may wreck one's health and looks. Most women are built like watches—one thing wrong upsets the whole mechanism.

Observing the small courtesies in life makes one charming. Knowledge of the various forms of society etiquette has made many women popular and has placed them in an enviable social position. Real politeness comes from a kind heart, from good impulses and it ranks as a strong beauty point because it illumines the face.

If one is obliged to work out for a living she must remember that habit affects looks. If one is energetic and happy the face will reflect the content. If one shirks her duty and hates her work, her face will reflect discontent; her vital organs will weigh downward and affect her health, and her looks will suffer. One must affect enthusiasm in her work to stimulate the vital organs.

So the real beauty is carved from within and the inward Sculptor is always at work. A girl is her own beauty doctor and can work out her own beauty destiny. She may have everything in life that she wills, if she will only guide this inner workman.

A girl who lives in the back woods may make herself so choice and beautiful in the indescribable way, that her fame will spread miles away. She should bide her time, stay to herself until she has fully improved herself, mind and body, and she will reap her full reward.

LAW OF ATTRACTION—VIBRATIONS

Everyone of us has a magnet within which attracts others for good or evil, and which is attracted by good or evil. The old philosophers have given us many proverbs to bear out this truth. We have the saying, "Birds of a feather flock together."

The law of vibrations was studied centuries ago by the old wise men. One attracts the kind of vibrations that one sends out. The Bible also has given us many commandments and injunctions to protect us from ourselves. We are told that one must love if one would be loved; "to cast thy bread upon the waters and it shall return to you," "as ye sow, so shall ye reap."

Whatever is projected returns sooner or later. One may not even send an evil thought as in an anonymous letter, valentine, or register an unexpressed wish without making herself liable to self punishment.

One's personality and thoughts, either good or evil, always surround her, "like a contagious cloud." A strong personality will influence a weaker personality just as a magnet attracts. Many are influenced because they vibrate similarly and many are influenced because they are attractable or weak.

Revivals, riots, political agitations and race prejudices are all evidences of the power of strong projections of thought. Race prejudice is the result of the vibrations of hate and anger sent out by strong minds. The world is what one makes it by the projection of one's thought. The magnetic, energetic, hearty person brings things about because he projects a stronger vibration of thought, will power and personality, whether in a hearty hand shake, sunny smile or display of interest.

By helping others we help ourselves. We must learn to give, give, give, in order to receive.

The sporting element and the under world recognize and fear the laws of vibrations. They know nothing of the laws but they have instinctive recognition of some force, which returns the act. They give because they desire luck. One may always receive help from them because they are afraid to refuse aid.

Washington Irving has said, "Happiness is a reflection." "Everybody's countenance is a mirror transmitting to others, its rays." If one makes a habit of sending out happy, loving thoughts, the face reflects the thought and gains in charm and beauty.

We must teach our minds to act upon the minds of others. We must learn the laws and obey them, that we may send out strong thoughts of peace and love to counteract the overwhelming tide of thought against us.

Love

There are many kinds of love. There is filial love, platonic love, the love leading to marriage, and the greatest love of all, mother love. Too many desecrate love by regarding it as a pastime, or selling all that passes for it, for favors, attentions and support.

What is love? Many definitions could be given but the best answer is, "Love is the habit of giving the best in us." Someone has said that "Love is the easiest thing to make and the hardest to keep."

So much of the life force is wasted because people imagine they are in love.

Somehow, girls are given to "falling in love," first with one man, then with another. With each man there is the feminine desire to reciprocate in full measure for various courtesies.

What is the result?

The vital forces are willfully wasted.

Beauty needs powerful stimulants. No one could expect a tree to blossom into a beautiful mature form if the sap were withdrawn. Youth is the green apple period. One can never tell how a little green apple may develop. It may become full blown and rosy cheeked, or it may become worm eaten and cankered.

Girls permit boys and men to kiss and fondle them (as one woman has said, "to paw and claw them") and in turn they exert themselves to live up to what they imagine is expected of them, believing it to be a fair exchange for gifts and attention.

When hypnotists desire to take the will power from their subjects they use their hands in strokings.

Girls should not permit young men to caress them, to hold their hands, or to stroke their bodies. It is very weakening. It causes a girl to yield to temptation because it induces passiveness to the will of the projector.

There is no present which a boy or man could give to a girl which is worth the tiniest atom of this precious invisible life current. In after life she realizes her folly, but it is then too late to remedy it.

Often a perfectly pure minded girl in her youth wastes her life forces with one beau after another, innocently imagining it to be her duty because of the attentions that she receives. When she marries the "man among men to her," she finds that she can not hold his affections because of this waste, and often she sees another woman get the love that is her due, as a wife. At the time of life when maturity should give a full blown rose of a woman, she has dribbled out because she has been too ardent. She is worm eaten and cankered because she has devastated nature, and it is all her own fault.

It is a debatable question whether a girl who has kissed many men, and has thus wasted her vital forces would be a fit candidate for Motherhood, and, on the other hand whether a boy or man who steals the life forces from our girls is fit to be a father. A man has no more right to steal this precious beauty stimulant from a girl than he has to steal her clothes.

Every man knows that if the girl he escorts around will kiss him, that she has kissed the one who preceded him and will kiss the one who follows him. It is no wonder that many men marry girls who have not seemed so promiscuous. Many a good girl has been passed or misunderstood.

Colored girls should never sell their bodies and they should set a higher value upon their bodies in every way. Especially should they be known as "Hands off" girls.

No one would think of handling a rare flower and expect it to endure. The virgin soul is always likened to a flower.

If a young man after a few calls thinks that he is entitled to a goodnight kiss he should be speedily set right.

Any emotion or feeling diffusing the body has an effect upon health and upon beauty. An organ may become exhausted from the rush of blood caused by an impure thought.

Kissing excites passions until they become uncontrollable.

A girl must cultivate her will power along with charm and personal magnetism in order to become a beautiful woman. She must resist the temptation to scatter her vital forces, so that when she marries she may hold all of her powers for the man she desires to hold. She should patiently wait for her "prince" and aim to give him unkissed lips, and virginity of mind as well as of body. It will be a tremendous satisfaction in fulfilling the definition of Love and Motherhood, besides giving the real beauty.

When boys and men desire caresses and kisses, a girl should send a message to her Solar Plexus—her reflex nerve—to help her to say, "No." She should let no present tempt her to be fleeced of her beauty food.

In order to resist temptation, girls should be taught deep breathing, that the diaphragm and educated nerves may obey emergency orders.

The practice of deep breathing is invaluable in the matter of resistance, and will back up the "I won't," "I won't," "I won't," "Hands off," "Hands off." A girl must hold her fists tightly and resist.

She must psychologize the mind with thoughts of resistance by practicing simple breathing movements, so that when temptation is imminent the holding of a deep breath will be her salvation. The action of her diaphragm and Solar Plexus will prevent any wavering.

To cultivate and hold vital strength, one must hoard every atom of vital strength. One may not even afford to write love letters in too warm a strain. One will not only be ashamed in after years when this particular fever has worn itself out, but one will then be conscious of wasted vital strength.

Beauty is so dependent upon vital strength that every atom of vital force is needed and none must be wasted.

Personal Appearance

Trifles show up the real character more than anything else, in clothes, or the care of the hair, teeth or finger nails. Personal appearance is one of the strongest factors in the beauty combination. After health, voice, and poise comes the value of dress as a beauty accessory. Dress has much to do with a man's classification of feminine beauty although he may not be dress informed. Many French women are considered beautiful because of charming dress accessories, which are generally immaculate and in harmony. A modest girl dresses modestly; a sensible person makes her clothes fit her person, her height, head, back view, side view, ankles and heels. A woman's dress soon tells the character of the wearer and betrays immorality. Even colors talk.

With many people, finery seems to mean good dressing, yet their clothes jar, cry out, even "scream out their unfitness and unwholesomeness, and betray their dishonesty, shame and sacrifice." Clothes show silliness, conceit, and selfishness more than any other thing, and often they shame a home, so a colored girl should study her individuality and her life position and dress accordingly. She should wear only becoming colors, and she might affect a certain color to her advantage. She should "cling" to what is becoming rather than follow exaggerated fashions. The exclusive dressers in high society study to get simple lines; with them severity in line is elegance. Such clothes wear several seasons. No one minds wearing a becoming style a long time. Few colored women can afford to keep up the pace of styles. There are women who live to dress no matter what the cost may be but they are not to be envied for this slavish passion.

A man wears a good suit several years and looks well. Colored women could plan their costumes that they might at least last two seasons. They should study to make the most of what they have on hand.

One good black dress still remains an asset to a wardrobe and most colored women look well in black especially if it is relieved by a becoming color.

In France only the "Boulevard" women and actresses wear the exaggerated styles that we see in the French fashion journals.

The Colored Girl Beautiful will take care of her clothes. She will learn to press and sponge, also the use of cleaning fluids, and to forbear from sitting carelessly on coats and other apparel.

Work clothes should be becoming in color and style. While one is buying or making she may as well select attractive models. When one is attired in unbecoming clothes, unconsciously the face reflects the thought in unbecoming lines. One's voice takes on a coarser, unbecoming tone, and the poise takes on an unbecoming attitude. For the same reason our girls should not wear men's old hats or paper bags on their heads.

One should aim to select something becoming that the face and body may always appear at their best. One must be on beauty parade ALL the time to get beauty lines.

Appropriate clothes should be worn at all times. Pink or blue satin or silk dresses should not be worn on Sunday or at church, even if one can afford them. It is bad taste and sets a bad example to poorer girls who sometimes sell their honor, even their lives for these perishable, inappropriate costumes.

In every mind there is a picture gallery of our friends and the people we meet. Sometimes the pictures that we carry are not the best ones. One is often caught unawares in soiled, unbecoming garments. It is not necessary in this day and time to give an ugly picture of ourselves.

We should be particular to give the best possible, most pleasing picture to others at all times. There should be no "being caught." One should be prepared early in the morning, anytime of day, and all through the night.

On the streets and as the street cars pass our homes, colored people should give the best pictures possible of themselves, if they can not of the houses in which they live. We are a poor people but we can be quiet, clean, becomingly and fittingly dressed. We must stifle the desire to be conspicuous unless it is to be conspicuous by quietness.

Deep Breathing

The Greeks are quoted as saying, "A healthy soul can only live in a healthy body." People are beginning to see that to a great extent, intellectual vigor depends upon physical vigor.

Man is an air breathing animal.

Air is life. One may go without food and water for days but not many minutes without air.

Air is the most important factor in generating vital force and it is the best tonic in the world.

A large, deep, chest indicates Health, Strength and Vitality. The size of the chest indicates the size of the lungs. A narrow chest indicates cramped lungs, heart, digestive organs and a small diaphragm.

The diaphragm is the dome shaped breathing muscle which serves as a partition between the chest and abdominal organs. Its contraction causes development of the lungs and heart and at the same time the internal massage of the abdominal organs.

The lungs have been called the scavengers of the body for they take off poison which would kill us.

As the blood stores oxygen especially at night, windows should be kept open to prepare the body for the next day's duties.

"Exercise is the elixir of youth."

Many people do not exert themselves enough to open the millions of little lung cells. Mother Nature demands a heavy price for this neglect of her laws.

The heart is now recognized as a muscle which needs muscular exercise as other muscles need exercise.

The heart is very wonderful. Although it weighs only about eleven ounces it has each day a lifting strength of 120 tons to the height of a foot. With seventy beats of a pulse a minute, six ounces of blood are forced into arteries seventy times a minute or 187-1/2 gallons every hour. This could fill a lake or pond in a life time.

Deep breathing is the fundamental foundation of Physical Culture, of Singing and of Oratory. This is why these studies are recommended to lessen the susceptibility to disease especially tuberculosis and other lung diseases.

Deep breathing cures nervousness and many chronic complaints because it improves the circulation of the blood and causes internal massage especially of the abdominal organs.

Deep breathers are seldom mentally weak because deep breathing develops Will power. Its study causes pride in one's body and its physical gifts because it teaches the values and beauties of different parts of the body.

The habit of deep breathing cultivates Personality and Personal Magnetism and thus makes one attractive. A great deal of the success in life comes from winning people through Personal Magnetism.

Originality

A woman's mind should always be filled with a life plan, else she is in danger. A busy woman is generally a safe woman. She must find her life work and keep busy. Even a hobby is better than nothing if time hangs on her hands. She should do something with all her might and not delay, for Time is flying.

A colored woman especially should have some purpose in life to further race advancement. It should not only be a high purpose but it should be something real.

To be enthusiastic about something is beautifying because it stimulates the circulation of the blood. Any kind of success comes from enthusiasm.

No matter how poor a woman may be she may be original in her ideas. At first, of course, she must use the ideas of others, until she can show her cleverness through her adaptations, and employing her powers and gifts will add until larger powers and gifts result.

She must try to get a new line of work for race advancement and dedicate herself to it. If she eliminates the Ego (Self) and will aim to work for the good of others, she will succeed.

Each one should find a realm, something in which she shall be supreme, and be first. "It is better to be first in an Iberian village than second in Rome." The race needs daring original people, to think and speak.

Emerson says, "Every man has a call to do something unique."

The person who thinks up new lines of study, thought and ideas for the race, enlarging its vision and enriching its mind is a race benefactor. Ruskin's creed of work should be the universal creed. "The man or woman who does work worth doing is the man or woman who lives and breathes his work; with whom it is ever present in his or her soul; whose ambition is to do it well and feel rewarded by the thought of having done it well. That man, that woman, puts the whole country under an obligation."

Colored women have a genius for leadership. There is great executive force in them. Many a colored woman is an undeveloped genius waiting for opportunity. One should try avenue after avenue until the right one opens, for her life work.

In spite of criticism she must fight on, alone if necessary, "With God, one is a majority," said Frederick Douglass.

If one can not be a genius or be original, she may do anything near at hand. She should find something to do so that she will have something to talk about besides herself and her friends.

One might take up the study of music, voice culture, elocution, art, embroidery or housekeeping (domestic science) and pass it along to others.

The surest way to make people "take notice of one" is to work for others. One may also live in peoples' hearts as well as their minds, if she will ally herself with a good humanitarian cause.

If one is not what is termed religious, or is lacking in religious feeling, she should at least conceal this serious void by showing respect for religion in no unmistakable terms for the sake of example. One should always hold up Christian ideals even though she may not be a spiritual woman or be called an earthly saint. She can hold up for a more rigid moral code and the highest thought in ethics.

It pays to be respected, but after one has trusted and has been disappointed, deceived, and betrayed, she will find that it pays best to keep close to the "Cross" where that "One always listens and understands." One should not get too far away from "It" because one is certain to return sooner or later.

The best representative people go to church if only for example's sake. Even if one were not extremely religious she could be an authority on religions, reading up the history of other churches as well as one's own church discipline. One might originate prayers or "graces" for the table and sell printed copies for a local charity.

Any woman should be proud to espouse the cause of children and their broader education, as well as their health and happiness. One might try to bring a musical artist or lecturer to them every two or three years.

Everyday of one's life there is an opportunity to make someone happy. One might amuse herself by keeping a diary of her efforts along this line.

Speech is a cultivated talent. One might study to be good company, not to be funny or witty, but she might study the art of expressing herself; not to air her knowledge, that would be vulgar, but to store her memory with a fund of information concerning the great paintings and works of art, and lives of great composers.

One might even be an authority on economy and demonstrate how to make over dresses, hats, etc.

One could economize on her wardrobe and travel on the savings giving little "Travelogues" to those less fortunate. There is an indescribable joy and satisfaction in serving others, even though the recipients are not grateful. It gives one a sense of power and wealth.

One might even cultivate her sensibilities and increase her knowledge of the beautiful in Nature and Art, to carry young folks upon little Nature and Art expeditions to the country or to museums. Permission might be granted to enter many closed doors. The word children is often an open sesame.

If one is tied down to life work inside her home, she may manufacture smiles and cultivate a beautiful speaking voice. It is a pleasant occupation to bring smiles to the faces of others. It is rather fascinating to try to change the expression of other people's faces by exaggerating the happy timbre in one's voice. Even if one may not do big things she may charge the atmosphere with smiles.

When I was a girl, an old friend used to say to me, "Never let people down you, always come up smiling." One may come up from troubles and bitterness with a forced smile until the smiling muscles act for themselves, automatically.

One may also cultivate good manners until she wins a wide reputation for real ladyship, and thus be an example. Only the uncertain are impolite; fear is their ruler. Those who own strength and power are always those who are gentle because they are sure of their life position. Real politeness is only an outward expression of the generous impulses of the heart; it is inborn. Politeness may be cultivated until it passes for the real thing.

Originality does not include exclusiveness. Exclusiveness is deadly to originality. The exclusive woman is seldom of service to the race, and she is not always a congenial or an agreeable person. She may live so much to herself that she is uninteresting as well as selfish. She touches nothing vital excepting books and has nothing else to talk about.

One should train herself to make a perfect social circle as far as she is able.

The display of wealth is never original—only vulgar—and only an inborn vulgar woman would place her so-called friends at a disadvantage by entertaining them beyond their power of return.

It is pathetic to watch the social efforts—"climbing"—of people with only money "Sans" brains and originality.

YOUTH AND MATURITY

The two attractive periods in a woman's life are girlhood and maturity. If girlhood is not sufficiently attractive a girl may go into beauty training for maturity.

Many women who persevere in right thinking and right actions have three stages of attractiveness, youth, maturity, and old age.

A face that reflects nothing is seldom beautiful.

To be beautiful one must think more, love more, in the right way, and give more in the right way.

A girl should not try to get old and look old, for age comes to her soon enough. Girlhood comes but once in a lifetime. One must keep young by being young and "thinking young." One must never let tiredness leave its mark either in the face or poise. Tiredness has never attracted and when people say that one looks tired, it is time to smile and deny it, for the "Spot" is beginning to take form. The body should never be permitted to settle. In Cuba, the women have enormous hips because they sit so much and are inactive.

Each muscular movement should reflect health and youth until one feels hardy and young. One should breathe all the fresh air that she can consume. Breathing is a vital force which sends blood to fill out wrinkles and eradicate blemishes and spots.

The fair, fat, and forty age is no longer dreaded. Like Lillian Russell, women are learning to keep the face youthful by keeping the illusion of youth and the belief that she is youthful. If we feel young we look young.

Self Control

W ill Power is the rudder of the ship of life."
    A woman's life is about what she makes it. She is her own
Fate. The law that governs one, governs all humanity, because the laws
of thought are the laws of the universe. The mind and body are co-
workers. "As a man thinks, so is he." Great men are those who see to it
that the mental force is stronger than the material, and who "Will" that
thought shall rule their world.

Every thought stimulates certain brain cells, and exercises some
nerve, tissue or muscle. Man's superiority to animal is due to this
mental action.

Actions speak louder than words. They are published thoughts.
Every movement of every portion of the body has significance.
Picking up a glass, a cup, or tools and other habits reflect the mind
and its superiority to the physical. There is no surer way to judge
people.

Every face tells a tale and we read character from the physical form—
the head, the backbone, the eye, the mouth, the chin, or hand. The
uplifted eye, the corners of the mouth, the manner in which one eats
or stands, in fact every movement has a special meaning, which may be
easily read.

The body is like a camera, it tells the truth; it is the outward sign of
inward grace, or vice versa.

Someone has said "Women's characters are writ large on their faces
and God writes a perfectly plain hand." Because women are more
emotional than men and because they often indulge themselves in
emotions, the signs are frequently very evident. If we study these signs
when we meet others we may "size them up," and almost know what
is passing through their minds. Because of sexual magnetism men read
women more easily than they read men.

Mental habits soon become reflective or automatic. In order to read
others we must study ourselves, discover our habits and tendencies and
trace them to their source for correction.

The time has arrived for new thoughts, new studies, and new habits.
Colored women must be led along the new lines of thinking. Although
many have seemed stupid about some of the abstract studies, they have
native powers that have too long lain dormant.

Many are permitting their forces to go to waste instead of controlling them. They must discipline themselves to gain self control over such habits as over-eating, coarseness, inertia, anger, and other beauty destroyers.

Any excessive emotion debilitates the nervous system and thus affects good looks.

Proper poise prolongs life because pressure on certain organs is evenly distributed and no strain is placed on any particular muscles to cause abscesses or tumors, etc. Improved circulation of the blood results, and good circulation spells health. One can think better when poise is correct for the same reason.

The conversation of people gives a pretty correct estimate of character. Complaints from people who are sorry for themselves is one of the tell-tale evidences of a weak character.

There is a present day need of knowledge concerning a certain contagion of emotions. Strong feeling sometimes vibrates that which is hostile and selfish. One fretful, scolding woman can upset a neighborhood, to say nothing of a household.

One's thoughts should be of love and peace, instead of worry and fear, lest she may harm others. A woman should be unafraid to conquer life's problems. She should have faith in herself or she will be a dreamer instead of a doer. She must be positive instead of negative, but be positive in the right way which includes the thought and help for others.

Voices reflect the mind and soul, so the colored woman should control the speaking voice.

Ella Wheeler Wilcox has said,

> "Some voices affect us like music,
> Some voices arouse to action and ambition.
> Some voices fill you with despondency.
> Some voices irritate like a buzz-saw.
> Some voices snap like turtles, and some hiss like serpents."

Control of the speaking voice is one of the most admired evidences of self control.

The power of the mind over the body is said to be greater than any germ. Compelling the mind to perform someone useful disagreeable act each day is a splendid habit trainer. The influences that we exert over others will depend to a great extent upon the control over our own habits as well as the resistance to influence that others might exert over us.

One must conquer habits of laziness, untidiness, extravagance, voice, gestures, clothing, to gain power to concentrate Thought.

Many girls think that they understand men, but they flatter themselves. Men do not always understand themselves, and often do things because they have been led to "the doing," by misunderstanding the girl.

A man likes to measure up to the opinion of sympathy, strength, protection, or wickedness, that he imagines a girl has of him. He often says and does things to please the girl more than to please himself.

Girls often throw out allurements and temptations especially in the way of immodest dress and seemingly innocent actions which have been the downfall of men as well as of themselves. While men have known that the temptations were deliberately planned, they have not had sufficient will power to resist. It is an unpardonable crime for a young girl to take such an advantage for frequently she ruins the career of a man. Such a girl has two souls to answer for when her own downfall is a sufficient burden to carry.

Some girls complain of insults from men. There are so many good reasons which could be given for this, but girls would indignantly deny that one reason is that they bring this upon themselves.

They discuss slippery subjects and personal experiences, and "heart longings" which call forth the ever present manly (masculine) sympathy. This often leads to actions afterwards regretted.

Men are good readers of the public bulletin—a girl's face. They see the mark of intoxicants, impure thoughts and other weaknesses as if they were spelled out on the features, and as they are keenly sensitive to projected vibrations, they act accordingly.

Sometimes dusk, or night's darkness is to blame for much mischief. Moral resistance seems to be at low ebb at this time, and an evidence of timidity or other feminine weakness may be misunderstood—read incorrectly as a feminine subterfuge seeking physical contact.

If one will always expect good from men—the men will generally rise to it. Try to believe that every man is chivalrous, but do not put his chivalry to too severe a test.

Curiosity and a too venturesome spirit may lead to mischief and trouble too great to be remedied. One must not think or project impure thoughts, nor must she expect insults and familiarities. Men generally

EMMA AZALIA HACKLEY

respond to the (influencing) thought. They feel the thoughts and obey them.

Girls must remember that most men talk. Some will tell on girls if it is the last act of their lives, although they may not mean to tell. A newly married man will tell his wife, or another will tell his affinity. Another may drink too much and grow confidential. Some even talk in their sleep. One may not think that she will escape; her indiscretions will follow her to her lifelong regret.

She should not try to be a woman too early in life, and should not marry too early. She should study her physique and her constitution. She should not permit desire and curiosity to control her good sense. Long illness, suffering, operations, and even early death may result from premature responsibility. If necessary, she should consult a physician and look the future squarely in the face.

Girls do not now mature as early as their mothers and grandmothers did, and they have not the same power of endurance and resistance, because times, conditions, and the mode of living have changed.

Long engagements should not be encouraged. If a man wants a girl he will wait patiently without any coddling or coaxing. Long engagements are enervating. Engaged couples feel that they are licensed by public opinion and they tax their powers in a way that married people would not dare to do. Too much liberty in long engagements is so often a serious menace to health and happiness in after marriage relationship. It takes away the charm and bloom of married life because the man learns to know his fiancee too well.

The Religion of the Colored
Girl Beautiful

God is the perfection in all that is good. God is the best in us. God is the perfection of all that is beautiful, orderly and harmonious— the 100 percent of everything in the world.

The religion of the colored girl beautiful should teach her that everything is spiritual—sacred—because everything comes from God.

It is not sufficient to say, "I am a Christian (I am spiritual—of the Spirit)" unless one expresses this in countless ways each day. Not only in kind, helpful actions and gentle speech, but in the work-a-day life.

The colored girl beautiful expresses her Christianity—her spirituality— the best, or 100 percent in her, when she puts Christ into every act of her everyday life. No act should be too insignificant for this expression.

The parables of Jesus teach us that He put His Spirit into the lowest act, as for instance in the parable of the tent-maker.

If the colored girl beautiful is truly of His Spirit she will spiritualize, light up her everyday environment with the "Light" that is in her as a beacon to others as well as to show her appreciation of a priceless possession.

Each day she has innumerable opportunities to express the Christ in her—her spirituality—in the neatness of her apparel, and in the tidiness of her home and yard. She may take her religion—her Christ— into the kitchen and express Him and the 100 percent spirituality in her cooking, sweeping, and in her dish washing.

Doing things well expresses the proportion of the Christ—the perfection—the 100 percent in us. The more Christ one claims, the better should one express Christ in his daily labor as everyday evidence.

A low daily percentage is a poor record for one who claims spirituality on Sunday.

No untidy church, home, or school expresses Christ—for Christ represents perfection in cleanliness and order. "Cleanliness is next to Godliness" we are told. Cleanliness shows the spiritual, the God, but dirt in any form is an expression of the opposite. Dirt under a bed and a prayer beside it are not compatible, to say the least, unless the "pray-er" is unable to sweep.

The Christ principles properly interpreted and applied would spiritualize a broom and duster and all the utensils of a home or the tools of a trade.

EMMA AZALIA HACKLEY

Order is an expression of the God-part which makes us more orderly in the habits of life if we make pretensions as Christians.

God is not only all that is perfect in cleanliness, order and harmony, but He is also all that is perfect in color and sound. God is in the body and all its parts, the hair, teeth—all.

As harmony and color are expressions of Spirituality so good taste in dressing expresses the God in us. By observing and studying Nature one learns God's taste in color and what is harmonious.

We should dress to suit the color of the face and the physical attributes that have been given to us. God has appropriately garbed each object in Nature. Colored people should study themselves and dress accordingly. The bright, gay colors are not suitable to all. Many violate the laws of harmony of color, and unconsciously expose the ugliest in their appearance by wearing gaudy, unbecoming, inappropriate clothes.

As the harmony of sound comes from God, so an eloquent voice expresses God. Christians should make their voices more elegant and eloquent. A loud, coarse voice expresses the opposite of God. Coarseness in thought and speech is unlike Christ and serves to reveal opposite attributes to those He represents. Grunting is not spiritual. No one could imagine a grunt from Christ.

A graceful motion or gesture also reflects the God in us. One would never imagine any rough, uncouth gesture from Christ, who is the "pattern of patterns." Grimaces are not spiritual besides they leave lines in the face.

A respect for the rights of others expresses the God in us, as do obedience and kindness. We are told in positive language by God to respect our elders and superiors.

Race pride expresses the God in us. The Israelites were the chosen people because of blood ties. They were proud of their blood. Blood is thicker than water. The real Christian should be proud of his people; he should believe in them and uplift them as our Great Example did the lowly.

The reverence which expresses God will cause one to respect His house or any portion of it. A Christian would not handle a Bible carelessly and would dust it as a privilege, because it is the message from God. A Christian would not tear or disfigure any sacred book or selection of music, while to sit upon the sacred rail of the altar or pulpit would be an unpardonable act of sacrilege.

The proper care of any article belonging to the Sacred Service is an expression of Spirituality because it recognizes the article as a medium of spirituality, something which should be reverenced.

The singing of religious songs in any but a spiritual frame of mind would be sacrilege just as the taking of the Lord's name in ordinary conversation or in exclamation is sacrilege.

The same religion or Spirituality which makes one shout, pray and sing should prompt a girl not to wear a pale pink or blue satin dress or other inappropriate fancy decollete dress to worship in God's House. She cannot worship God and mammon at the same time and she should not be the means of distracting anyone from spiritual thoughts through envy or disgust.

The Christ in a person will prevent her from speech and action which would hurt the chances or success of another person. God has warned us that the violation of this rule will surely return evil to the violator. His law has many references to this particular self punishment.

It can not be denied that Divinity has specially endowed the Negro spiritually, but he does not consistently express it in all the forms that he might express it, especially in the great Race cause. He is full of heart, and will give his money, his food, his life, for God—but he does not yet realize that the same love for God that he puts into his gifts should be expressed and applied in his daily walks in life as Christ has expressly commanded.

We are taught that there are four kinds of Emotional Expression: The Egotistic which is self and in the interest of self as in joy, rapture and grief; the Aesthetic which has its expression in Nature and Art; the Ethical which has its expression in the moral law; the Religious which expression is in the faith of the Supreme Being.

As yet the Negro has only fully expressed himself in but two: The Egotistic, or the self interest, and the Religious, or the faith in the Supreme Being.

The Negro undoubtedly brought about his own freedom through his own spirituality, and faith, and the concentrated, united thought of a whole people upon one subject—freedom. His remarkable progress since emancipation has been due to the same faith.

The Negro should be, and could easily be the spiritual teacher—or example—of the world. He must not only prove his spirituality but he must diffuse it, that others may realize its power even if they may not receive its benefit.

Christ, the Supreme Example of spirituality was quiet. Other races hold that ideal, of spirituality. When they see and hear a Negro shout, weep and pray and then find that same person uncouth and dirty, they cannot reconcile the two conditions, and so doubt the spiritual element which they call Emotionalism. (They do not remember that the Spirit may be strong and the flesh weak.)

These critics cannot believe that an untidy, ignorant man with dirty teeth stained with tobacco juice can give spiritual advice, and one must admit that it does look incompatible.

The race needs more quality in Emotion and less quantity.

Once convince the rankest Negro hater that the Negro undoubtedly has spirituality, which is surely advancing him and the race, and a certain respect will follow.

Each Negro must consider himself a spiritual missionary whose appearance, speech, actions and surroundings will reflect the storehouse of the great Light within.

The colored ministers who preach Emotionalism, or what they term the expression of spirituality should see to it that their flocks spiritualize their daily lives causing cleaner churches, schools, homes, yards, wearing apparel and Christian thoroughness in each daily act, thus showing 100 percent spirituality.

The colored ministers who preach Non-Emotionalism should prove that the power of spiritual expression is being directed along channels which are helping their flocks and the race in each daily act, not only in race progress but in convincing doubting Thomases who are blind to the good traits in the race.

The so-called Spiritual Power which would cause a woman to run down an aisle and mash the hats of others, or to throw hand bags and give similar evidences of strength and emotion could be turned into safer and more helpful channels—as far as her race is concerned. A woman possessed of this power and energy could be a great leader in great deeds if she were taught how to do this. A shouter who can not help the race in the battle against prejudice in her special locality, by expressing her spirituality in each daily word and act as well as apparel, and surroundings, seems a poor example of spiritual expression.

The religion that does not help toward the advancement of this persecuted race, and does not win the admiration and respect of other races, is not the religion for the colored girl beautiful, of today.

As a rule colored people expect entirely too much help from God. We must help ourselves more. Each Negro carries a three-fold burden; first, his own personal burden; second, the burden of his posterity; and third, the burden of the race. These follow each other and are dependent upon each other.

God has given him physical strength, a strong backbone and strong shoulders to carry the heavy yoke of the three-fold burden, as well as a wealth of spirituality to cheer him and keep his heart light, along the way of life.

The religion of the Negro should prompt less study of the desires of the personal Ego, and should teach other nations to respect his race, or, his religion is not spiritualizing as it could and should spiritualize.

The religion of the colored girl must be spiritual in every sense, that it may influence her every thought and act, and make her a true medium for race progress.

The School of the Colored Girl Beautiful

E ducation is the process of developing all man's powers, physical, intellectual, moral, aesthetic and religious for the proper discharge of the duties of citizenship."

The school that the colored girl beautiful should attend will have trees, grass, flowers, shrubs and a garden (even though a small one) that the girl may keep in close touch with the first teacher—Mother Nature.

The care of the school campus as well as the windows, fences, and surroundings, will reflect the careful spirit of the school.

The colored girl beautiful will select the school which fights flies, dirt, filth around back doors; the school which aims for sanitation before putting in electric lights; in fact, a school which has health and sanitation for its hobby.

She will attend a school that buys books and takes care of them and which compels the students to read that they may grow into the reading habit, to pass it along to posterity.

The progress of the race will depend not upon the "book learning" taught in schools, but upon the right habits formed and the amount of self culture that the school inspires.

The colored girl beautiful will be taught to keep her eyes open and her mouth shut that she may never betray how little she has really learned in her preparation for the real school—the school of Life.

The colored girl beautiful will be taught her duty and relationship to the race, that she may be a living example of what right education and right training will do. She will study human needs and about the history and progress of her people that she may take her place in the affairs of her race if called upon, and then bequeath her knowledge and good qualities to succeeding generations. She will be taught lessons of self-control and modesty; to respect her womanhood and to conduct herself that she may command respect from all men and boys including those of her family.

She will be taught enough of the world to step into its arena knowing the evils to shun. She will be taught to hold out a helping hand to weaker ones who may succumb to evil.

She will aim to live in pleasant relationship in the school that she may acquire the habit of living in peace in social circles and neighborhoods in the scheme of after life.

She will be taught that politeness is a necessary virtue; that every form of impoliteness is an evidence of mental as well as moral weakness and that an ill bred colored girl is a curse to the race. She will be taught the value of silence and that of speech, and will aim to train herself along both lines for silence is often more effective than speech.

She will learn that the aim of education is the aim of religion, that is, to lift one above the animal. She will endeavor to lift herself to the highest plane of true womanhood that she may pull others higher.

Colored schools are supposed to correct the tendencies of children who have lived under careless, untidy conditions, and to give them ideals of cleanliness and order.

She will do her part of the school work cheerfully and thoroughly, that she may know how work should be done, and how to train others—her children, perhaps, if so favored.

The colored girl beautiful will be taught the value and use of money, and the relative value of character, education, and other things, which money cannot buy. She will be taught the care and cleanliness of the body, simplicity of wearing apparel and appropriate becoming inconspicuous costumes for church, school, street and home.

She will be taught that fine clothes can not cover up bad manners, nor take the place of good character; that it is foolish to buy what one can not afford; that the expenditure for clothes especially should be gauged by one's salary and should be appropriate for her particular plane of life.

The laws of proportion in the scheme of life must be the hobby of the school for the colored girl beautiful.

She will be taught that it is unforgivable not to walk erect, to talk in good English and in a soft tone of voice.

As many girls fall into book ignorance after graduation she will be taught that the aim of education is to give good habits of reading along with book-knowledge—or else the school has failed to educate a colored girl beautiful.

The colored girl beautiful will not aim for book education alone. She will select a school which will fit her to grace her home from parlor to kitchen, a school which has thoroughness for its motto.

She will be taught how to make her dresses and hats, to prepare for the time when perhaps her allowance for clothes must be divided among several. Dressmaking is a science as well as an art and enough

EMMA AZALIA HACKLEY

can be learned, by those not apt, to save many dollars—especially in the home that fate favors with children.

She will be taught a trade, or some means of earning a livelihood, that she may be prepared, if circumstances should force her into the business arena.

The school of the colored girl beautiful will so educate her that motherhood will be her highest ideal in life, the glory of colored womanhood.

THE HOME OF THE COLORED
GIRL BEAUTIFUL

The Home of the Colored Girl Beautiful will reflect her. She will help her parents to buy a home that it may give her family more standing in the civic community. Taste and simplicity will rule, for the home will harmonize with the girl. If her parents are not particular about the trifles in the way of curtains, fences, and yards, then it must be her special task to make the home represent the beautiful in her, the God, for all that is beautiful and good comes from God.

Windows generally express the character of the occupants of a house. The day has passed when soiled or ragged lace curtains are tolerated. The cheaper simpler scrims and cheese cloths which are easily laundered are now used by the best people.

The Colored Girl Beautiful, will study the possibilities of her home and will attempt to secure the restful effects for the eye. Too much furniture is bad taste. The less one has, the cleaner houses may be kept.

The ornate heavy furniture and the upholstered parlor sets are passing away because they are no longer considered good taste, besides they are too heavy for cleanliness and are harmful to the health of women who do their own work.

Furniture of less expensive model, with simple lines and of less weight are being selected. These may be paid for cash instead of "on time," as has been the custom of many people in smaller towns and in the country districts.

The furniture sold by the payment houses always shows its source in its heaviness and shininess.

The wall paper should be selected as one would select a color for clothes, to harmonize with the color of the skin in all lights, and, for service Color schemes in decoration are being followed and we have no more stuffy parlors, often closed for days. Instead we have living rooms, with cleanable furniture, strong but light, entirely suitable for winter, and cool in summer. No one has a parlor now-a-days. The best room is generally a living room for the whole family. No more do we see enlarged pictures which good taste demands should be placed in bed rooms and private sitting rooms. The ten cent stores have done a great deal of good in educating the poor white and black alike. These stores have everywhere sold small brown art prints of many of the great paintings, to take the place of the gaudy dust ladened chromos and family pictures.

Pictures are hung low that they may be thoroughly dusted, as well as to give a near view of the subject.

Expensive carpets are also things of the past. Painted and stained floors with light weight rugs are more generally used. These may be cleaned and handled without giving the backache to women. Many colored girls boast of having painted their own floors and woodwork. Much of this has been learned in the boarding school.

A tawdry home expresses its mistress as do her clothes.

Next to the kitchen a fully equipped bath room is now the most important room in the house. Health and sanitation are the topics of the hour and a colored girl should know how to put a washer on a faucet as well as her father or brother.

A house without books is indeed an unfurnished home. Good books are the fad now. They are everywhere in evidence in the up-to-date colored home. They are exhibited almost as hand painted china was. In every inventory or collection one finds a Bible, a dictionary, and an atlas.

The times are changing and the colored people are changing with the times. Cleanliness and health are the watchwords, and "Order" is Heaven's first law.

The Colored Working Girl Beautiful

N o one should ever scorn a colored working woman. She has been the bone and sinew of the race. She has built the churches, helped the schools and has made the race what it is. The pioneer colored woman in most instances has helped to make the wealth that many colored families enjoy, today.

In my travels, on entering Southern towns early in the morning, colored women are the only women seen on the streets, and sometimes the only persons. They hurry along often with insufficient clothing in cold and rain.

One thinks of the little ones at home who dress themselves and perhaps, younger children, all without a mother's care, until night when the tired woman's return to her home to cook, to wash and to iron for her family after a hard day's work, in service.

In the antebellum days some of the Negro working women may have been lazy but their descendants of today are not lazy—only fifty years after. Statistics prove how many homes have been bought through their labor, how many children are sent to school. Working women pay the family doctor bills, and support the churches and charities.

"Every person should work or else she will need a doctor." Habits affect looks. If one is energetic and happy in doing her work, her face will reflect the contentment. If one hates work, the face will reflect discontent, the vital organs will grow flabby and affect the health, and looks will suffer. Enthusiasm in work stimulates the vital organs, causes circulation of the blood and makes the eye bright and the skin to take on a more healthy hue.

If a girl is obliged to work in a kitchen she should respect her work and dignify her position. She may be a "Somebody" washing dishes or scrubbing a floor, if she does not depreciate her work and if she will give it status instead of half doing it and complaining about it.

Only a somebody "can" work well. We cannot get blood out of a turnip, and neither can a nobody "do" things. A slip-shod, half-hearted working woman is a curse to the race, because she gives it a bad reputation. She should put the "somebody" stamp on every portion of daily work and do the work as if she expected to get a diploma for it each night. She should not work mechanically or it will be drudgery. She should put pride and enthusiasm in her work, and let it reflect her inner self.

EMMA AZALIA HACKLEY

It is the duty of every working girl to make her employer adore her for her personal value and her word. "Do so much better work than you are paid to do that not only your employers, but their friends will take note and soon you will be paid for more than you do."

Be ready for the opportunity or crisis which is bound to come in a change for the better. Stick to a position like a leach. Make it a bigger and better one than you found it and it will prepare you for greater openings. Somebody is always watching good workers.

In her relationship with men the colored working girl beautiful will put a higher appraisement on herself than may be necessary in the case of the more fate-favored colored girl who stays under her parents' roof. Because she works is no reason why she should be cheap, easily attained, or easily pleased as far as men are concerned.

She will demand much instead of little from men, that they will offer more for the privilege of her society. Unless she is engaged she will be wise to permit no caresses and will try to conquer the tendency towards accepting "petting."

She will bide her time for the recognition of her worth. Many a servant girl has seen her posterity lead a town, socially.

To know how to wait is a great secret; to patiently bide the time when one may step into the niche that right living and preparation has made possible. She will try to be contented and will strive for power to conquer her work, and herself to be ready for the day when opportunity will open her door to a larger and more responsible life. The beautiful part about this is that she will be ready to fit into this new condition of life.

She should observe, listen and imitate the good when at work. Contact is often worth more than money. Many valuable lessons have been learned while "in service." While alone working one has opportunity to "think" and Thought rules the world.

A colored working girl is a racial trust. Her race burden is a heavy one. Her speech, actions and diligence constitute the measure by which the whole race is judged.

One need not permit previous family conditions or disadvantages of birth to hamper her progress in life. No matter what one's people have been or are, one is not to blame providing she rises above all of it.

She must "get up" and pull her family up after her, if she can. If this can not be done she can pull herself up—up—up and be the "somebody" in the family. She may grow in character, influence and reputation, until people will forget her ancestry and any objectionable relations as well as all former environment.

The Colored Working Girl Beautiful should not fear or worry about what people may think. She should save her money. A bank account is always the most respected thing in the struggle of life.

Even if some single black deed threatens to blot out the whole of a good life (in one's own case or in the estimate of the world) she should be brave enough to live it down. One should put her personality into everything she does and "do" things worth while. The world moves on so fast that even the bad is forgotten soon. One may live anything down nowadays if one tries.

If she may not go with good people socially, she should stay alone. In time she will make herself and others believe that this is her preference.

She should not push or try to climb; she should bide her time. In the meantime she might improve herself; she might study the piano, elocution or singing, and prepare for the day when opportunity will open the long-closed social door.

The Colored Woman Beautiful

In spite of everything to be said on the subject the womanly woman is always the strongest magnet whether she is called beautiful or not.

If the colored girl has not been taught by her mother or guardian to train herself for a beautiful maturity even after she has passed girlhood, it is not too late to train herself.

Good begets good, so she will exert herself to make a wide circle of friends altho she will be careful not to grow too intimate with any. She may be a real friend without undue intimacy.

It is conceded that most women "must talk" to someone but too much intimacy means too much freedom and this often destroys friendship.

One cannot argue, quarrel, or criticize and still expect real friendship. One definition of a friend is, "One you know all about and still like." One should not try to "make her friends over" and one never says disagreeable things to her friends nor does she make unfavorable comments about their personal attire or weaknesses. She lets her friends learn all unpleasant things from others. "The links of the chain of friendship are held by a very delicate thread." The tiniest word, doubt or action may sever the links.

The colored woman beautiful will try to love that she may be loved. She believes that "man is his brother's keeper" and she has ideals and visions for the race. She has a moral obligation; she reaches out a helping hand to others. She can mix without being mixed. We can not help others unless we mix. There must be close contact—touch to lift up others.

The colored woman beautiful believes that everyone who gets up must pull up, or else she will be kept down by the weight of the racial burden. Each one's welfare is closely bound with that of the masses. The race as a whole must progress and prosper, or else no unit may prosper. The colored woman beautiful gives the best in her for race advancement. She works, thinks, and reads to be ready for the need of the tomorrow and its problems.

The colored woman beautiful will not carry "chips on her shoulder," looking for slights and insults. If she carries the thought too strongly it becomes catching and someone will take up the idea. She will set into motion lesser vibrations in the minds and bodies of others and the things she imagines will happen.

She should resist thoughts of suspicion. She must not think about the things she wishes to keep secret, for thoughts are contagious.

The colored woman beautiful does not call another woman "bad" just because she does not measure up to her ethical code. She must be so persistent in being good herself that everyone else seems to look and act good. If God loves the lowest, she can afford to do likewise. She follows the rule, "Judge not that ye be not judged." She does not make the mistake of criticising those who have not her strong will power, lest having stronger projection this unkindness may return swift and sure to her. To permit the absent to be disparaged or depreciated in her presence is almost as harmful to herself as if she had said things.

What is "good" in (another) woman? What is "bad" in (another) woman? These are two difficult questions to answer and a woman must not judge by her own standard for herself. Women are inclined to be too narrow in their viewpoint in judging other women. While one may boast of her virtue of virtues some women may have a bundle of lesser virtues of which to boast. It takes more than one virtue to make a good woman. Many women are unduly vain of their escape from the "sin of sins" and some of these may have known no temptation.

When one notes how many good friends a so-called "bad" woman may have, one wonders why it is. Those who understand the law of vibrations recognize that the woman has projected something of herself which has brought her a rich return in spite of her one weakness.

It is a terrible thing to be a bad example along any line to young girls, so every colored woman should try to conquer herself and live down any weakness or error. She should give out the best that is in her that she may be a good example to younger women. She lets the light of love and purity shine in her face and transform it, and it will reflect in the faces of others and make her own soul the happier.

EMMA AZALIA HACKLEY

The Colored Wife Beautiful

M arried life is a co-partnership and the wife and husband pledge to mutual help, when they enter into the marriage contract.

If in their girlhood wives had only studied men instead of giving up all their time to so-called "loving and courting," there would not be so much dissatisfaction, heart-ache and complaint after marriage. A girl should try to select a man with control over himself, over his voice, his emotions, even the angle of his hat, and then she should practice control herself, until the two dispositions have become adjusted to each other.

The ignorant girl who marries is full of trust and inexperienced notions. The disillusionments of life seem to come too fast to suit the majority. Many young wives immediately become discouraged or desperate and fall out of the ranks by the wayside of the matrimonial highway, without trying to live up to their end of the contract, or even respecting their own vows at the altar.

"True loving is giving the best within us." When we have company we give to them the best food, the best linen, the best china and silverware that we own. Yet to those we are pledged to love and cherish we give anything, and wonder why in return we have failed in receiving love and all that goes with it.

A divorce is a terrible "something." It is a blight to children and often means their ruin or the blasting of their future. If a woman has children she should try to endure her lot until they are grown. In the meantime she may prepare herself for a beautiful maturity and an entrance into the commercial world or another field of activity.

Of course, if one's husband deserts her there is nothing else to do but let him go, but if he clings to her and the home, she should use the protection that his name gives to her until she is sure that she can buffet the world alone.

In the larger field of public life a woman without the protection of a husband's name has a hard lot if she has physical or other attractions. Widows of both kinds are always under suspicion. If one is lighthearted and enjoys even innocent pleasure, she may be called a "good timer," or "fast," and this may injure her advancement in the arena of business life.

The protection of the name of any kind of a man, bad, no account, or cruel, is better than the suffering from cruel suspicions which often blight the efforts of a sensitive woman, who perhaps in her loneliness has turned for sympathy this way and that way, until she concludes that if she suffers in name she may as well be "in the game," and chooses the wrong way.

If a woman has money it is quite different. People fawn upon her and she is less liable to snubbing if Dame Gossip should assail her.

The first duty of a wife is to keep healthy. Even if she is ailing she must not complain unless through mental suggestion she desires to increase her ailments, real or imaginary. She must earnestly endeavor to discover the cause of the alleged ailment and remove it.

The colored wife beautiful of today must be a composite woman because the colored man of today is many sided. They call woman a "creature of moods" but most men may easily be called susceptible and changeable creatures, when it comes to the attractions of the opposite sex.

Today it may be a pretty face which allures him; tomorrow a fine conversationalist, or a musical person may attract. The next day a woman with tremendous vitality may charm him. So he wanders, but he does not intend to stray. One or several streaks in his make-up have been satisfied, but his wife still stands upon her pedestal as the woman who bears his name.

The up-to-date wife realizes his susceptibility (as a man) and is prepared. She bides her time when like the prodigal, he will surely return, perhaps mentally and morally purified and a wiser, if a sadder man.

If a woman loves her husband and desires to keep him for herself and family, she must train herself for her many varied duties including attractiveness, which is a real duty.

If she thinks that someother woman has her husband's affection, her thoughts help her to make this so. If she voices the suspicion she fertilizes the soil and aids the growth or she may crystallize and give form to rumor.

Even if there is ground for such a suspicion the up-to-date wife would not admit it to herself or voice the fact.

"Man's love is of man's life a part, 'tis woman's whole existence."

The inexperienced wives forget that they cannot satisfy every mood of a man without study or effort, unless they are remarkably gifted. Many a wife has neglected her mind, body and powers and when some woman with developed powers enters her marriage orbit, she flies off at a tangent, admits defeat and gets a divorce without putting forth an effort to win back the husband who is often worth saving.

It is humiliating to admit, "I have lost my husband!" A wife should never admit it, even in thought.

Many a man does not intend to stray and loves his wife but he has been carried off his feet just for the moment.

There are Keeley cures to save men, why not husband cures to save homes, especially those with children whose futures are at stake.

I know several colored women who have had good ground for doubting their husband's fidelity who have never allowed the men to know that they have doubted them.

One wife made a study of "the woman in the case" and threw her and her husband together in her home until the man was satiated. In the meantime she studied herself and the woman to see what it was that attracted her husband. Then she went into training for the match—war—if it should come to that—in attractiveness, and she won without telling her secret.

If a wife will give a man time and will play the attractive game as she did before marriage, her husband will soon turn his face homeward, and will wonder what the other charm was.

Many men are attracted by youth alone and after youth has flown they are not interested. A wife should study the fancies of her husband if she desires to hold him, and then begin work upon herself, to hold her youthful looks.

Wives must prepare for the dangerous age which they say comes to a woman between thirty-five and forty-five, and to a man from forty to fifty, when both are accused of being attracted to younger faces, and when they do foolish things. A wife must strengthen herself, lest she stray, and cultivate her own attractive powers lest her husband should incline to stray.

A man does not age as quickly as a woman. At fifty a woman is supposed to be on her decline while a man is in his prime at fifty.

It is a woman's own fault if, at forty the lines in her face turn down and if her hair and teeth are all gone. If she is a "nagger" the reflection will appear in her face. If she has permitted household cares to swamp her, and reflect themselves in her face and body, she has no one to blame but herself.

Many a woman has attracted her husband through her singing, conversation, or other accomplishments and after marriage has permitted these to decline, and has not lived up to the ideal that she gave him before marriage.

A wife should ask herself if she is living up to the ideal she suggested before she married, or if she is a disappointment, before she questions her husband's conduct.

Some wives think that their morality in wifehood is all sufficient. A woman may boast of her "virtue" until doom's day, but "if her soul is small and her heart stingy" her example is not worthy of imitation—for she is only good to herself. She has no way of proving the ownership of the "virtue of virtues." It takes many virtues to make one "good," in the real sense of the word.

A colored wife should not be discontented without good cause nor should she complain of monotony when she may choose so many helpful diversions, and may help to make others happy.

Every colored wife who has not borne children, or a wife who has lost children owes a duty to the children of others.

In fact, these owe a greater debt to posterity than the mother. Such women should not live for themselves alone, lest they canker. Contact with youth infuses youthful thoughts and enthusiasm, and keeps a woman's heart young, and if her heart is young her face will reflect this mental attitude.

There are thousands of children with living mothers who still need "mothering." One may work out her own youth and beauty culture while "mothering" a little one. It is worth a trial as a youth stimulant.

There are four great laws given to a wife:

"Brace up! Brush up! Clean up! Look up!"

The Colored Mother Beautiful

When a woman enters into the marriage contract—into the partnership of home making—it is understood that parenthood is to be the chief aim and hope.

If a man is good enough to marry and to contribute his support, he is good enough to be a father or else he should not have been selected.

A woman who marries and does not intend to have children is merely an object of convenience who has sold herself.

To assume the position of colored motherhood is the greatest privilege and responsibility that can come to any woman in this age.

The colored mother beautiful carries a heavy burden—the weight of future generations of a handicapped, persecuted people. She may bless or curse each succeeding generation; she may change race history; she may make a more beautiful race with the beauty that comes from beauty of character and right living.

What a privilege to carve the destiny of a race! How glorious to look into the future and see lines of ancestry influenced and advanced by her thought and example, to see her stamp of personality upon a posterity which will point to her in pride and thankfulness!

The time has come when each colored girl must prepare herself for this rare privilege, when she must distribute her powers and talents for race good.

Whatever the colored mother is, millions of colored children will be. A colored mother lives not only for herself and for her own children, but she must live for the race. A colored mother is a success as she measures up to her relation and obligation to the race.

Negro children of all children need mothers who are strong spiritually, physically, and intellectually. Enough colored children have been born under bad or careless conditions. The child born under bad conditions can not be expected to hold his own among other children.

No woman has a right to blight the future of her race. Not even her body may be abused—this beautiful casket—the treasure house of future souls. Any crime that she commits against herself or her body she commits against the race.

Almost any colored mother would lay down her life for her children but she must have a wider vision into the scheme of life and the world, and must deliberately plan to make her grand-children and great grand-children healthier, happier and more useful.

While it is admitted that heredity is not all, yet inherited tendencies have great influence.

The colored mother beautiful must be a living example of all that is progressive. She must study more about the laws of heredity, and child culture to prepare the child for its race battle, unhampered by inherited mental or physical tendencies.

The "gray matter" in the colored woman's head is the same as the gray matter in any woman's head. Through the exercise of will power she may conquer inherited tendencies and even command nature as other women are doing.

There are many books which will guide and instruct a prospective mother who should read and learn all she can on the laws of reproduction. She should absorb this knowledge that she may be able to impart it to less informed women.

The early Romans are said to have surrounded a prospective mother with examples of courage and strength.

The mother of Napoleon is an example of the power of pre-natal direction. She is said to have studied military tactics and to have visited battlefields. The mother of Michael Angelo is said to have watched the painters of pictures in the Cathedral. The result was the greatest artist of the time.

As mental impressions are as active during the night as in the day, no prospective mother should carry unpleasant thoughts to bed. The sub-conscious mind receives the bad thought at bed time and acts all night under this influence. Its forces affect the same as thoughts during the day.

The prospective mother should read good books, think right, live right, and keep a pure mind and heart, thus developing a deeper nature to bequeath.

More than anything else, the prospective colored mother must practice self-control. All worry is poisonous. Strong thoughts of disgust and hatred if not controlled during the pre-natal period are liable to leave disastrous affects. The aim should be to train herself to change any thought which will create a physical disturbance.

Mothers who fail to control their tempers, passions, and indulgences too often weep bitter tears as they see in their off-spring the consequences of their own wrong doing.

Someone has said: "Parents transmit deviltry to children and then punish them for it." Instance after instance of such cruelty could be cited. Why should parents expect their children to be better than they?

Anger causes a chemical change which acts like poison to the system of an adult. It affects the heart, stomach, blood, and nerves and causes many other disturbances.

"Often the unborn child's little organism is flooded with shocks of passion and disturbed by nervous movements which cause unsound mind and body."

Altho inheritance comes from two lines of ancestry, the prospective mother may be able to control and supervise the tendencies from her line. She must do all in her power before the birth of a child to sway it for good. She may then save herself years of worry and sorrow and the race an unworthy example.

Before and after birth the colored mother beautiful will cultivate and give out the best in her. No contrary or selfish thought will be permitted because of the bad effect upon the child. These unpleasant things will enter soon enough into its life. The mother will faithfully endeavor to be an example to her children in thought, poise, speech, personal appearance and in all forms of cleanliness and politeness.

A child's ideal seldom goes higher than that of its mother. Children very accurately reflect the thought of their parents.

How can the child have high ideals and elevating thoughts unless the mother has them?

Taste is said to be a faculty of the soul. The mother bequeaths her taste.

How can the colored mother beautiful expect her children to have habits of observation and appreciation of the beautiful in Nature, Art, Science, Music and Literature, unless the mother has "walked and talked with nature, has heard the tongues in trees and brooks" as Shakespeare has said, and has pointed these out to the child?

If the starlight, the moonlight, the dawn, the sunrise, the sunset, the blue sky, the tranquility of a summer day or the grandeur of a storm have no response in the mother's soul, then how can a child be expected to lift its eyes and see the beautiful everywhere, everyday and absorb the benefits from such communion?

The physical feeding of a child occurs but three times a day but the spiritual, mental and moral feeding goes on all the rest of the time. Children should be fed ideals of thought and affection to counteract the evil effect of thoughts of passion.

The colored child should be taught to think and should be given opportunity for a quiet hour for self communion and self entertainment. It should be taught to live a period of solitude so that in after life it may not always be compelled to hunt around for entertainment and excitement.

How can the child be expected to love reading if the mother does not read to it?

How can the child love music if the mother does not play or sing to it or teach it songs?

How many nights are wasted that might be spent in giving colored children ideals of home life and right habits in reading and home study?

Colored children have been left alone too much.

How many of them have a children's hour? How many have been given something to think about? How many spend their spare moments in reading? How many can recite poems or give quotations from the master writers?

The mothers themselves must put sometime in exerting their minds in reading and thinking with a view towards mentally improving the next generation. They must observe and note what is passing on in the great world. History is being made everyday. How can the child resist the desires of the lower nature when its mother has tantrums? The colored mother must refuse to express passion. A mother can not shame or beat her child into gentle manners when she is rough or coarse.

How can the child be careful and controlled in speech if the mother has not the power of expressing herself in good English. Language is too powerful a weapon in reaching, compelling and swaying the feelings of others and in winning friends—to be neglected.

Children always betray home training. If they have not been trained properly as they are not adepts in dissembling and they reflect their mothers in all their thought, speech and actions.

The mother who is strict in her own conduct and who pays careful attention to the home conduct of her children will seldom be ashamed of their deportment. Good habits may not be assumed at a moment's notice. The good breeding of parents is very truly reflected in the manners of their children.

It is sad to have the children learn the laws of politeness and good breeding outside the home, and to watch them assume that which should be innate.

It is sad to hear little children lie about their home training pretending that "My mother makes me do this or that" when they know that the mother has failed to make a strong point of this particular fault.

It is sadder still to hear colored children say, "I can't." The colored mother should put success in the child's thought and teach it to believe in himself and his race. It is the duty of every mother to preach success and one's duty to aim to excel along all lines.

How can the child be clean and love cleanliness when its mother is habitually untidy and slovenly? The colored mother beautiful would no more exhibit herself unclean than naked. She would no more walk slovenly than to dress slovenly. If a mother wears unclean clothes, has unclean thoughts or unclean manners, her children will reflect her.

How can a child hold her head up and her back straight when her mother slouches around and forgets that her body belongs to God as well as her soul.

The colored mother beautiful makes a point of teaching her child to be true and helpful to the race, and to speak up for the good points and keep silent about the weaknesses when before other races. Every race has strong and weak points.

She should take part in efforts for the advancement of the race. No one can lift the race unless he stays in it. A child should be taught not to depreciate the race anymore than it would itself.

No one is so big and strong that he can exist alone. All of us are dependent to a degree. Each one will need friends. There are no friends which mean so much to us as those of our own race.

The percentage of physical deformities in colored children is lessening. Colored mothers are learning to study children's faces and bodies in order to change and correct their physical defects. Bowed and weak legs, outstanding ears, misshapen mouths, noses and teeth are being corrected according to scientific rules. Then, too, they are training children to do things to improve their own physical defects without— of course—causing them to be over conscious.

The colored mother beautiful is the health officer of the race as well as her own posterity. It is her duty to see to it that her children have clean bodies inside and outside. She will see to it that in her neighborhood there will be more regard for health, drainage, and other sanitary conditions. She will pursue the deadly fly and cause this pest and all vermin to be eradicated.

She will study up on the kinds and amounts of food to give children that they may not be fed the coarse, greasy food which coarsens the instinct, or may make them gluttonous, which will abuse the stomach and cause unnatural heat that may wreck them morally. Instead, she advocates the light brain forming food to lift them above the dominant animal tendencies.

She controls the child's play which is so necessary to health and which at the present day aims for educational results.

A colored girl's estimate and idea of colored womanhood comes from her mother.

The colored mother beautiful will not give the best to strangers in preference to home folks, nor will she expect her daughter to receive politeness from other boys and men when her brothers and men in the house keep their hats on, smoke and talk in loud disrespectful tones before her.

A colored mother will teach her daughter to command respect from all boys and men and not to capitulate in anyway. To do this she will teach her daughter that she must conquer or control her lower nature and not permit privileges with her body or her given name. Her conduct at home and on the street must also command this. Her daughter will no more use the Lord's name in exclamation than any other profanity. She must be taught not to hang out or talk outside of the windows.

She must be taught that she is never to stand and talk to men on the street, also that she must not continue a conversation with a man or boy who shows he has no respect for her. She will demand a respectful attitude if she is a good girl or else she should excuse herself from further conversation and association.

The daughter of the colored woman beautiful will be taught to expect boys and men to tip their hats in meeting and parting, and she will not encourage them to sit in her presence if she stands unless they are her elders, superiors, or invalids. If necessary she will exaggerate the importance of these seemingly small courtesies to impress them upon other younger and less thoughtful girls.

Such a daughter will be taught to count for something besides clothes and looks. She will pass an intemperate or immoral man as she would something polluted, for both are irresponsible and she may suffer from even a moment's contact.

This daughter must be taught not to marry for support or for money. That is selfish and cowardly. Love should be the basis of marriage because after the honeymoon is past there are responsibilities, troubles, sorrows and self-sacrifice which need the stimulation of the "Love light."

The daughter of the colored woman beautiful will aim to marry a man mentally and physically fit to be the father of her children. An immoral, vile-tongued, untruthful or diseased father is a curse to his race. It is her duty and aim to improve racial stock.

This daughter will study the ethics of the period of engagement and will not abuse or destroy the mysterious charm which belongs alone to the early period of wife-hood.

A girl should be taught the duties of married life; to fulfil the beautiful aim of motherhood should be her ambition and her daily prayer.

Boys, also, get their estimate of colored womanhood from their mothers.

A whipping, striking, scolding, threatening, "shut-up" mother presents him a wrong view point of real motherhood.

The colored mother beautiful will teach her son to respect colored womanhood and to show this respect in every word and action. He is not supposed to know the "wheat from the tare." To any woman in all the small courtesies of life he will reflect his mother's home training. He will be taught to look up to, and to show special respect and reverence for the great women and men of the race.

Even in the way he puts on or takes off his hat he reflects his mother.

If a colored boy is expected to tip his hat to any woman, he should tip it to the women of his mother's race.

If it is expected that he should stand erect before any woman, he should before the women of his mother's race. Off will go his hat, if even asked a question. His voice, his eyes, his backbone, his heels, all reflect his mother and her training. In spite of protest he will never sit if a woman is standing unless he is ill or a cripple. Especially does he exhibit the mother training he has received from his manner in his actions to colored women.

If he is expected to speak respectfully to any woman he should to the women of his mother's race.

If he works faithfully for any woman who employs him he should work faithfully for a woman of his mother's race.

When he marries he should select a woman of his mother's race—a Colored Woman. His mother will teach him that a good wife is about the best thing in the world.

He will be taught to support and trust his wife as he did his mother and never doubt her until he has positive proof that she is unworthy.

He will never publicly put another woman before his wife if he lives with her. As long as a wife bears his name and stays under his roof she is entitled to the respect that her title is supposed to carry. He would never go about complaining of his wife for that is small and cowardly. He will tip his hat as gallantly to his wife as to another woman and kiss her with uncovered head to show his respect to the woman he has chosen to bear his name.

The son of the colored mother beautiful will not smoke in the presence of his wife or friends unless he is sure it is unobjectionable and he should regard this as a privilege rather than a masculine right. He will be taught to wear his coat at table and regard it also as a privilege if he appears otherwise. He will be taught that it is unmanly to tattle and gossip.

He will be taught that it is vulgar and low to quarrel especially in the home. No man will strike a woman no matter what the provocation might be anymore than it would have been right for his father to strike his mother. A man who is unable to control himself in anger is a weak man and is hardly fit to be a husband, much less father. Belonging to a race full of impulse and emotion he must be taught to control his emotions as he would his appetite. Culture and manliness are really restraint.

He will be taught to remember the vital sex difference in strength and physique and will not permit a woman to lift or reach unnecessarily— not even to help with his coat. He will not preach a double standard of morality for the men and women unless he practices what he preaches and has always been pure.

Early in the boy's life the colored mother beautiful will teach him to keep as pure in thought and deed as girls are expected to be. He will be given a right idea of the sacred sex organs and will be taught their health—value and the price of their abuse. Self mastery will be the watchword in thought, even in sleep and recreation.

The colored mother beautiful will teach her son not to lie and steal or to use intoxicants and profane language. She will teach him to keep both his inward and outward body clean. She shall insist that he keep his lips "in" while his chest will be out. The son will be taught the value of a good name and that fondness for work is one of the best recommendations in the world. He will be taught not to scorn or neglect his chores and to help his mother in the housework, not only because it is his duty but because it will prepare him for the duties of married life when he may be able to help his wife or instruct her if it should be necessary.

The colored mother beautiful will teach her son to be a little man and not to receive "penny tips" like a beggar. He should be taught to do neighborly favors without pay, after first asking his mother for permission. If he must have money let him work for wages that he may be his own business boss. He should never be permitted to ask anyone but his parents for pennies and he should be encouraged not to expect or accept them.

A boy should be expected to walk with a graceful carriage and present an attractive personal appearance in the way of clothes, teeth, hair and nails as well as a girl.

Early in life he should be taught to invest in a savings bank, to get the saving habit.

The habit of reading good books should be made a part of his daily work as a preparation for the idle hour when he would otherwise seek excitement and harmful association.

A boy should be taught the duties of married life and what to expect from a good wife.

He should be warned of pitfalls and how vicious girls and women play upon men's physical weaknesses for selfish purposes. Any abuse or excess may ruin his health and happiness.

He should be taught to appreciate the qualities in a girl which will make congeniality during the long married life which has trials of which courtship never dreams.

He should be taught to seek and appreciate good, respectable girls and to associate with the best people.

If the day should come to the colored Mother Beautiful when after years of patient sacrifice and toil, all her hopes and dreams are cruelly dashed to earth and the child so carefully nurtured refuses to do her duty to parent and race and will not help to make the race and world better by having lived in it, or, when perhaps, the child is a disgrace to her parents and the race, the mother must conceal her agony and grief and still keep a serene countenance.

In silent meditation she looks back over all the years in which she has tried to rear a creditable member of the race and society. If, after honest review, down in her heart she can truthfully say, "I have raised my child to the best of my knowledge," then she may leave the rest in the hands of the "Creator." Perhaps he will reward her efforts, in a future generation, while she is yet on earth.

A disappointed colored Mother Beautiful does not envy other Mothers nor does she criticise their daughters.

Suffering opens the door to a wider vision in life and if she looks around she will find forgetfulness in helping others. It is never too late to begin.

Perhaps the Colored Mother Beautiful will be spared to see the day when her children leave the home honorably. Although it almost breaks her heart because she is no more to be the guiding light and comforter, she yields the sceptre of authority gracefully and willingly and steps into the background. She may see a rough voyage ahead for the young life travelers, but she may not interfere nor advise these loved ones unless asked. Even then she remembers that experience is the greatest teacher and strengthener and that it is best for them to walk life's journey alone.

The peace and contentment that comes from having done her whole duty gives her a spiritual beauty of countenance that comes from the other world; the habit of right living through right thought, reflects in her face and gives her a physical beauty that comes in no other way.

At the last, the Still Small Voice Whispers, "Well done, thou good and faithful servant of a persecuted race. You have done what you could. No one can do more. Receive your eternal reward," and the face is illumined with the beauty that shall endure forever.

A NOTE ABOUT THE AUTHOR

Emma Azalia Hackley (1867–1922) was an African American writer, teacher, singer, and activist. Born in Murfreesboro, Tennessee, she began taking piano, voice, and violin lessons at a young age. Despite her light skin and hair color, she refused to pass as white in order to streamline her musical career, preferring instead to put her heritage at the forefront of her personal identity. She graduated from high school in 1886 in Detroit, Michigan, where she had moved with her parents several years prior. While working as an elementary school teacher, she married attorney and newspaperman Edwin Henry Hackley, with whom she would move to Denver, Colorado. There, Hackley founded the Colored Women's League and the Imperial Order of Libyans, taught music to countless African American students, and earned her bachelor's degree from the Denver School of Music. In 1905, she divorced her husband and relocated to Philadelphia, where she worked as musical director for a local Episcopal church. Hackley, who founded the Vocal Normal Institute in Chicago in 1911, was highly regarded as a teacher, working with such artists as Marian Anderson, Roland Hayes, and R. Nathaniel Dett. In 1916, she published *The Colored Girl Beautiful*, an etiquette book for young African American women.

A NOTE FROM THE PUBLISHER

Spanning many genres, from non-fiction essays to literature classics to children's books and lyric poetry, Mint Edition books showcase the master works of our time in a modern new package. The text is freshly typeset, is clean and easy to read, and features a new note about the author in each volume. Many books also include exclusive new introductory material. Every book boasts a striking new cover, which makes it as appropriate for collecting as it is for gift giving. Mint Edition books are only printed when a reader orders them, so natural resources are not wasted. We're proud that our books are never manufactured in excess and exist only in the exact quantity they need to be read and enjoyed.

bookfinity™

Discover more of your favorite classics with Bookfinity™.

- Track your reading with custom book lists.
- Get great book recommendations for your personalized Reader Type.
- Add reviews for your favorite books.
- AND MUCH MORE!

Visit **bookfinity.com** and take the fun Reader Type quiz to get started.

Enjoy our classic and modern companion pairings!

Classic & Modern

www.ingramcontent.com/pod-product-compliance
Lightning Source LLC
Chambersburg PA
CBHW020604030426
42337CB00013B/1211